You Won't Always be This Sad

a Book of Moments

SHEREE FITCH

NIMBUS
PUBLISHING
— NIMBUS.CA —

For Everyone!
In Faith
Sheree
2019

Nimbus Publishing Limited
3660 Strawberry Hill Street, Halifax, NS, B3K 5A9
(902) 455-4286 nimbus.ca

Printed and bound in Canada
NB1500

Mary Oliver quote from "The World I Live In," published in *Devotions*, Penguin Random House.

M Travis Lane quote from the poem "A Gift from the Bad Fairy," in *That Crisp Day Closing on my Hand: The Poetry of M. Travis Lane*, published Wilfrid Laurier University Press.

Quote from C. S. Lewis from *A Grief Observed*, published by Faber and Faber.

"Let This Darkness be a Bell Tower" from *A Year With Rilke*, translated and edited by Joanna Macy and Anita Barrows. Copyright © 2009 by Joanna Macy and Anita Barrows. Reprinted by permission of HarperCollins.

Editor: Whitney Moran
Cover design: Jenn Embree
Design and Illustration: Peggy & Co. Design Inc.

Library and Archives Canada Cataloguing in Publication
Title: You won't always be this sad : a book of moments / Sheree Fitch.
Names: Fitch, Sheree, author.
Identifiers: Canadiana 20190162724 | ISBN 9781771088398
Subjects: LCSH: Fitch, Sheree. | LCSH: Parental grief. | LCSH: Bereavement.
Classification: LCC BF575.G7 F58 2019 | DDC 152.4—dc23

Nimbus Publishing acknowledges the financial support for its publishing activities from the Government of Canada, the Canada Council for the Arts, and from the Province of Nova Scotia. We are pleased to work in partnership with the Province of Nova Scotia to develop and promote our creative industries for the benefit of all Nova Scotians.

Again, because of you, Dustin.
And, as ever, for you, Jordan.
Because of my *anam cara*, Gilles, who walks the labyrinth with me
at every turn.

To my mother,
Dolores Shirley Comeau Fitch,
Mother of joy and sorrows,
for wisdom
which sustains me
moment
by
moment.

Let This Darkness Be a Bell Tower

Quiet friend who has come so far,
feel how your breathing makes more space around you.
Let this darkness be a bell tower
and you the bell. As you ring,

what batters you becomes your strength.
Move back and forth into the change.
What is it like, such intensity of pain?
If the drink is bitter, turn yourself to wine.

In this uncontainable night,
be the mystery at the crossroads of your senses,
the meaning discovered there.

And if the world has ceased to hear you,
say to the silent earth: I flow.
To the rushing water, speak: I am.

— RAINER MARIA RILKE, *Sonnets to Orpheus*

What is clear is that meaning may not be something we find. We found no meaning in our son's death, or in the deaths of countless others. The most we could hope was that we might be able to create meaning.

— ELAINE PAGELS, *Why Religion?: A Personal Story*

Because you know, Mama, you can't lose the music.

— DEE

CONTENTS

PREFACE

You cannot save people. You can only love them.

— ANAÏS NIN

What happens when, despite everything you've tried and done and done and tried and prayed and cried and loved and done and tried and cried and prayed again, you wake up one day in your usual I-can't-take-it tear-streaked runny-nosed way and really know – I mean k-n-o-w in your head and heart and in every cell and tissue and toenail – you know, the truth is that the ones you love most, hold closest, hold dearest, those who are carved in your heart, those who you live for, those who you would die for – are in pain?

And you cannot heal them.

You can do nothing. Except, maybe, pray without ceasing.

What is prayer if not hope?

But what happens when hope dies?

Love. Well, yes, just keep loving. Others, yourself, the world.

Sometimes easier said than done.

What happens to any of us when the story doesn't work out the way we dreamt of?

Or when we find ourselves trying to keep our head above the quicksand that is grief?

My son Dustin died at age thirty-seven on March 2, 2018. A few weeks later, with his three-year-old daughter asleep beside me, in the middle of the darkest night of my soul, at the bottom of my deepest sorrow, I discovered overwhelming gratitude. A gratitude unlike any I had known before.

I was swallowed underground that night, and it was terrifying there, excruciating; it was my own version of Dante's Inferno.

When I couldn't take another breath, I had a profound experience of *oneness*.

> *At grief so deep the tongue must wag in vain; the language of our sense and memory lacks the vocabulary of such pain.*
> – DANTE ALIGHIERI, *Inferno*

There is no way to explain what cannot be explained but I'm as certain as I could ever be that I came very close to seeing, knowing, feeling this world through the eyes of the Divine, to feeling the broken-heartedness of the whole world – past, present, and future. How beauty and horror coexist. Yes, there is darkness.

But there are legions of angels and spirits who weep with us, protect us, guide us.

I see now how we, the living, dwell amongst the dead.

I was already in pieces, fragmented, undone. In shock. But this was another threshold.

After that night, I felt like a newborn in an unpredictable world.

Yet there is clarity in the unfathomable landscape of loss and sorrow.

There are voices there, and visions.

At the very bottom of my deepest sorrow was gratitude. How could that be?

Write, said my dear friend, Deanne Fitzpatrick. *Write*. She has been my muse more than once.

You are a writer. I want to hear what you have to say.

I listened. To her. And to the silence.

The pen was heavy to lift. Then it became a wand of healing. A way forth. I wrote, wrote, wrote.

This book happened because an editor listened, too, as I chronicled moments in that first year. As I sculpted, sorted, scored them.

Moments, because I see the word *mom* in moments and because for a while I lived, not day by day but breath by breath. I wish I could say that is an exaggeration. But anyone who has lost a child knows, it is not. Time disappeared. So did the sun.

I read, read, read. As if books could save me.

Some of these pieces were written in real time; some were meditations and writings sparked while studying through the Abbey of the Arts. Some arrived while on retreat at Seaton Spirituality Centre in Terrence Bay. Many were responses to things I read. Some arrived or were finished after the first anniversary of Dee's death. (I will just call him Dee. It was the name he called himself, the name tattooed over his heart.) This book, however, is not about him. Not really.

These are my psalms of broken-openness. Lament, praise, and thanksgiving. Prayers of a kind. A book of devotions. Fragments. Utterings. Confessions. These words are the touchstones that tell a fractured story of a year.

Like the building of a labyrinth by the man who chose to be Dee's father. Beneath the hot summer sun, on his knees, my husband, Gilles, created a sacred place. Rock by rock. This, a man diagnosed two years ago, at sixty, with Alzheimer's. He is proof a person never forgets love.

I'd walked a labyrinth when we lived in Washington DC. I had been studying theology again, served occasionally as a healing lay minister at the Washington National Cathedral, beginning a lifelong apprenticeship as a "wounded healer." But I'd forgotten the practice of labyrinth walking until one night, as I sat in the deep pit of darkness, I heard a voice. Not Dee's voice or the voice of God, but the small voice inside we have to learn to listen to. That small voice said *labyrinth* and I stopped crying and I said yes, yes, labyrinth, a labyrinth, that is what we will do, we will build a labyrinth for Dee and I will walk there and it will be good.

I try to walk our labyrinth twice a day. Each time, I am convinced the ground beneath my feet becomes more solid. I am learning, with the help of a teacher, how vast emptiness can become luminous emptiness. I will always be learning.

And so, these moments are organized into three sections that echo the way of the labyrinth.

Releasing, walking into the labyrinth.

Receiving, pausing in the centre of the labyrinth.

Returning, leaving the labyrinth.

There is no right or wrong way to walk the labyrinth. And of course, I've discovered the truth C. S. Lewis observed in his grief:

> *For in grief nothing "stays put." One keeps on emerging from a phase, but it always recurs. Round and round. Everything repeats. Am I going in circles, or dare I hope I am on a spiral? But if a spiral, am I going up or down it?*
>
> *How often – will it be for always? – how often will the vast emptiness astonish me like a complete novelty and make me say, "I never realized my loss till this moment"?*

I know words can heal. Heal as in "whole." I hope these fragments, written in the rawness of the aftermath of losing my son, bear witness to LOVE as I explored and experienced my sorrow and my fear. For, like C. S. Lewis, I never knew "that grief could feel so much like fear."

How to be fearless? Again, I read and read. Books save me.

"Let your curiosity be greater than your fear," wrote Pema Chödrön, one of my favourite wisdom writers. "Fear not," was the message from the faith traditions I grew up with.

But this kind of sadness IS terrifying. *Don't stay sad, stay curious,* I kept telling myself. Still do.

So as I began to observe, I started to trust my mother's promise: *you won't always be this sad.*

Reader, I can only tell you this: I do not weep because of death, because there is no death.

I weep because of love. I dwell in the Mystery.

Such a beautiful sadness you will see, if you walk with me a while.

There are gifts and joy in the midst of it all.

SHEREE FITCH
MARCH 11, 2019

INVITATION

Beyond a pasture –
where
two sheep
three donkeys
three horses
graze

– there is a labyrinth
not a maze

in summer's heat
all on his own
a husband placed
each breathing stone

designed a place
his wife could roam
to grieve their son
to weep him home

now others walk there
spiral round
in so much love
on sacred ground

each rock a tear
the father shed
for every child

the
lost
the
dead

now

humble path

of rock and grass

welcomes pilgrims

all who pass

reeling spirals healing
circles

enter
one and ALL

INVOCATION:
A MOMENT OF PRAYER

           May the Spirit of LOVE
guide my intention
as I surrender
open
before mystery
bear witness

           May the Spirit of BEAUTY
surround me
in my search for gifts
of earth and sky and sea
for honest words
to offer in the blaze
of my remembering

           May the Spirit of TRUTH
surround and protect me
help me shed all fear
as I stay awake
in the darkness
of mourning
until morning
arrives.

Now, **breathe.**

RELEASING

What makes us think the heart breaks once? It breaks
all day. It breaks like rain. All that I did
not want to bear has to be born, and what I mend
has to be mended all over again.

— M. TRAVIS LANE

Sun

dances

on the tidal river

light

bounces

Spirit's silver-shimmer

Nature's glory-glitter

everywhere

on a Friday afternoon in March

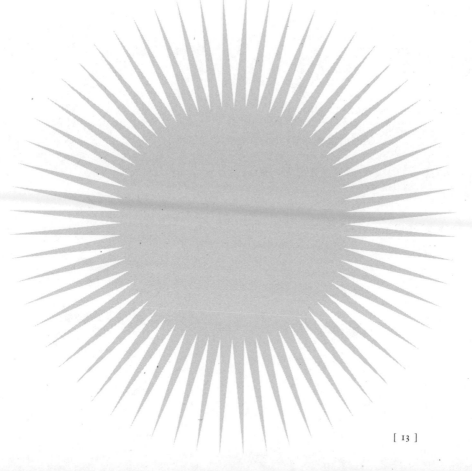

Work's almost done

met my deadline (for once)

so hey I'm

one

hip-hurray!

glad-hearted

woman

grateful for

this solar gift of light

shifting polar heaviness

a soul-lifting

energy surge!

welcome after the grey grim dirge-like days

of winter's weary-worry

green's still hiding underground
        yet underneath in musky darkness
trusty earthworms squirm
        Asian beetles hornets ants bluebottle flies
wake up
    with a doozy of a hibernation hangover
swarm the warming
              windowpanes

  surprise!
      their busy buzz a song
to say hello, again
    yes, we're **alive so very alive...**

    bliss in all of this
            perhaps a hope
for early spring?

   Phone rings
A number I recognize, know by heart

I pick up smiling, chirp a chipper

HI, YOU!

exhalation
    choking
– hello?
– hello?

strangulated
       wailing
            my name in raspy gasp
my name in rusty human static
    clipped words hiccup out
mutter out stall-stutter out
    incoherent rattle babble
syllable slip trips staccato –
a-a-a-am   bu
lance

                       p o ohh
                       lice –

where who
       he Dee
           was staying
a body
      carried

out on a s   t   r   e   t   c   h   e · r

– so, so he's what, he's at the hospital?
– no, he's
– what?
– he's
– what?
– he's
– what?
– what?
– what?
– he's

D

    d-ea-d   d

d_{ee}

    d_{ee}

        d ee

Circles of sound
surround sound
spiral round earth to ground
as if from another realm
another room
from another woman
one with a ripped-open womb
then wood snap-crackles
sound of fire smell of smoke?
clang of a blacksmith's anvil
announcing the arrival

Enter:
devil of death
a warped dark-hooded creature

It holds an ember-tipped
smouldering
poker in one hand

Brands
sizzles sears
a dartboard design
into my belly
my navel
the bull's eye

Death's dart
hits the target
pierces
sticks in place

N

O

o

Ooooooooooooooooooooooooooooooooo

o

o

o

OOOOOOOOOOOOOOOOOOOOOOO

o

OOOOOOOOOOOOOOOO-O-O-O-O-O-O-O-O-O-O-

In his workshop, across the road

G hears my siren shrieks

some otherworldly tortured creature's keening

starts running

bursts through the door breathless

rips the phone out of my hand

– what is it? who is this?

here I am / here I'm not

split in two – no – splintered

into

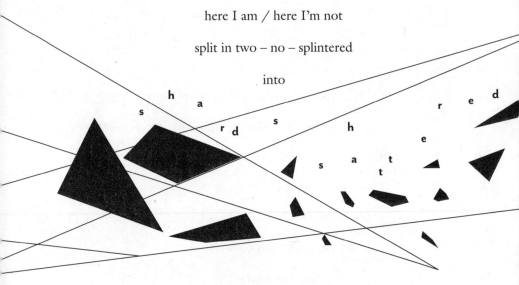

h
a
s
r
d
s
h
r e d
e
s a t
t

then there is this: a floating

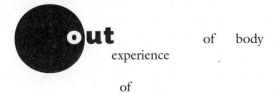

out of   body
experience

of

looking
down

watching myself   outside somehow

down on hands and knees

rocking

back and forth   back and forth

trying to breathe

screaming into the river

as I **push**

push

push

push

push

bearing down

the end of a long labour

helping him through yet another tunnel

as he struggles towards light

gone

to...   where?

Hovering. I hover.

Seems I know how to float in mid-air. Feels like treading water.
Now I'm doing the breaststroke, just watched myself down there
racing outside, on my knees on the ground at the edge of the bank
overlooking the river, the river still screaming in my ears, now
watch as I run to a room, yank open a drawer in the bedside table,
a sachet of lavender and beside it, yes, there it is:

Ten clear glass beads linked to a small silver cross. A piece of my
mother-in-law's rosary.

Rosary?

When she died, each of her children received sections of her
rosaries to keep.
Her name was Marie-Jeanne.

Mother of ten.

Yes, she is the first Mary to appear –
Ma belle-mère and there! Grand mère
Beautiful mothers, come to me.

Twenty minutes after the phone call, there's an RCMP cruiser in the
driveway. An eternity he's been out there, idling, but now we hear
his heavy footsteps on the porch
G opens the door. Mr. Mountie peers in, sees me:
                    – oh, he says, oh, you already know
Relief on his face as he swallows
his Adam's apple bobbing up and down
he's first to say, with genuine feeling
                    – I am so very sorry for your loss
I believe him

He's young. Maybe thirty-seven, same age as Dee, I think
then dearGodwhatifhehadbeentheonetoknocktotellus
                    – what a horrible thing you have to do, dear
                    tell people that someone they love dies
                    I am so sorry you have to do this, dear
I think I say that
        or something like that.
And I'm staring at his uniform –
the banana-coloured stripe down the leg of his navy trousers –
        I want to touch him.
He will smell of Old Spice, just a trace, a smell that means
        everything will be okay
        everybody will be safe.
        – My father was a Mountie
        maybe I tell him that, too.
                            Dad. Dad. Daddy.

Suddenly I am

little little little

but my father's dead, too.

my father in a funnel
of blinding white light
framed in an

arms outstretched

like a U in the word
h U g

in greeting

Yes, yes, Bumpy would be the one to be there to welcome you

if that's the way things really work

Suddenly I want it to be so

            heaven

like in the illustrated Bible of my childhood.

            paradise

        somewhere up there, waaaaaay up, yep yep

         my father, my brother, my son

together

in the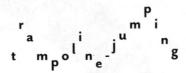

    clouds

or maybe

    in a meadow

        by a stream

        below a field

           where russet apples grow

Me now wishing they'll be going fishing now all kerfuffled hear the
shuffle-shuffle deal the cards for a game of crib 15-2 15-4 now cling
clang ring bang: horseshoes? Horseshoes! It's the RCMP's musical
ride! Intermission time now pum pum pum pum pum
in the gym hey y'all, basketball game of hoops holler whoops!
Ah hell. Heaven smells of sweaty sneakers gym socks baby powder
clam chowder
coconut cream pie

die

did you

die

did you

why

did you

how did

you

die

I am still getting smaller
                  – this is the number
Mr. Mountie interrupts
my shrinking thinking
                        brain pain panic
search for heaven

        – what number?
        – the coroner's office.
        – was there a –

— no   note

Dial tone
tone-deaf
dial
die all
the number.
– Medical Examiner's Office.
Try to speak.
Cause of Death?
Had he relapsed? Overdosed? Suicide?
– he was in an agitated state you see, I say
all his life, I want to explain
ever since he was six, I want to scream

– and he was so depressed these last months
trying to come off methadone
but there was no note

– if it makes you feel any better, she says,

it doesn't look like it was intentional.

Her voice a cushion of kindness
for my pounding head
a quilt of tenderness for my
shivering shivering shivering shivering
I can't stop shivering

– we will take good care of him, I promise.

Then I understand. His body is there.

His *body* is in a morgue.

I'm in some forensic television show

I see
body bag
stainless steel table
blunt instruments
toe tags
dead bodies in drawers of a giant filing cabinet

no! he was claustrophobic, I want to tell her.

do I smell something like...iodine? ether?

His body...

I-need-to-see-him-
eedtoseehimneedtoseehimneedtoseehimnee
oseehimneedtoseehimneedtoseehimneedtos
imneedtoseehimneedtoseehimneedtoseehin
eedtoseehimneedtoseehimneedtoseehimnee
oseehimneedtoseehimneedtoseehimneedtos
imneedtoseehimneedtoseehimneedtoseehin
eedtoseehimneedtoseehimneedtoseehimnee
oseehimneedtoseehimneedtoseehimneedtos
imneedtoseehimneedtoseehimneedtoseehin
eedtoseehimneedtoseehimneedtoseehimnee
oseehimneedtoseehimneedtoseehimneedtos
imneedtoseehimneedtoseehimneedtoseehin
eedtoseehimneedtoseehimneedtoseehimnee
oseehimneedtoseehimneedtoseehimneedtos
imneedtoseehimneedtoseehimneedtoseehin
eedtoseehimneedtoseehimneedtoseehimnee
oseehimneedtoseehimneedtoseehimneedtos
imneedtoseehimneedtoseehimneedtoseehin
eedtoseehim

I-need-
to-see-
him-

– you can, she says

– you can, you will.

dial tone tone-deaf dial tone

I must have said goodbye   BUT   I

didn't say goodbye

who found him   where was he

His body. My baby's body. My baby.

Yes, baby. I said baby. Because he was. He is.

Because every mother's child is ever
all the ages they have ever been
or might have been

I go to the safest place I know

        An autumn afternoon
            my brother and I
        buried under a dome of leaves
        bursting out, leaves swirling

        after, my father twirling us around
        our shrieks our rosy cheeks
        earth's damp-dark cellar smell
        trees twisted roots wind's minty tang

        this shimmering peculiar light

        look there, between
        a crosshatch of branches
        a glimpse of blue
        a jigsaw puzzle sky, o joy
        new baby sister's coos
        my mother's laughter

           yes

The Leaf Place, remember The Leaf Place, Mama? Mama!

I call my mother
my mother
alone in her kitchen
eighty-one years old
alone in her kitchen
my mother who has lost
a husband and a son
so many others

Mum Mum Mum

all I say

she knows she just knows
like she always
      knows
alone in her kitchen
his grandmother
                         all

      alone

Friends leave whatever they are doing
rush to our side as soon as they can,
the next Marys to arrive.

We gather in the living room LIVING room. Living rooms.

How many times the room where we speak of death?

These Marys gather us in their arms.
These Marys weep with us, breathe with us.

I keep forgetting to

breathe, that is.

Midwives.

Here they are, helping me through the waves of pain
worse than any contractions – yes, midwives to the death
of my child

their faces glowing
such beauty
in the anguished face
of empathy

Yes, Beauty.

surge of
gratitude
impossible
magnitude
the rush
in me
hush in me
a waterfall
washes over me
warm summer rain strange paradox!
because now *in this moment*
my Mary midwives
rescue me from

drowning

In this uncontainable night
of the endless first day
when we reach out
curl
into each other
weeping
I remember
a recent conversation

– a few weeks back, I whisper
out of the blue,
he said to me, softly

    – you know, Mum,
    don't you
    you know I'm going to die
    before you?

    – don't, don't say that
    – no no, I don't mean that
    would never do that to you but Mum

    you know I've done a lot of damage to my body
    you're going to bury me.

– So much certainty in his voice, a kindness even
as if he was trying to let me down gently

I said no, no I won't

fled the room

But he knew, I think he *knew*

I did know, too
somewhere in that place of knowingness
the crows that day on my walk in January
three hours plowing through snow praying all the while
sensing coyotes hiding in the woods watching me
I couldn't understand what I was feeling
but I know now: *Foreboding*

That is what knowing without knowing
feels like

– shhh. go to sleep. shh try to sleep…

try to sleep we need to sleep

– He must have known

been sicker than

he let us know

and this morning I woke up, moaning

praying out loud, I mean before I was fully awake

out loud, I prayed, I prayed that…

I cannot finish this thought

– shh try to sleep…

try to sleep we need to sleep

– shh try to sleep…

try to sleep we need to sleep

but we stay awake

as he

holds me

as he

always has

holds me

as I hurl

holds me

as I howl

to the moon

as I howl

louder than the wind

howl until I am hoarse

howl until the coyotes

across the river

howl back

in their holy

but ungodly

chorus

On the way to Halifax
where he died.

Drive-by sightings.

Signs on the highway advertise self-storage.

Self-storage, I almost laugh, *I wish.*

There's no place to put all this
this mess of a gutted woman
even if there were
there's no lid just like no goddamn Tupperware lid to be found.
    Or burped.

No baby to hold.
No baby to burp.
Why am I thinking of him as a baby?
Why am I smelling a newborn baby?
Why is that place he laid his head on my shoulder aching?

Turn on the radio
sing like a crazy woman
to SiriusXM Satellite Radio
Lollipop Lollipop oh lolli lolli lolli
Lollipop!
laugh like a crazy woman

oh, the absurdity
Life I mean
Self-storage. Lollipops. Death.

Snapping my fingers to a song
at a time like this

how the road stretches ahead of us

have you ever noticed how the power poles
are like giant crosses on the highway
& there are so many white wooden
crosses in the ditches
marking where
someone's
loved one's
died?

Christ died for our salvation.

Whatever.
My son is dead.
Will you save me from that, Jesus?

I don't think so.

Still, once more
I clutch the rosary
will not let it go
know I will hold it close
in the hours, days, weeks, months, ahead
in my wallet
in my pocket
panic when I cannot find it.

I do not even know how to use it.

– *Teach me*, I ask her son, the very lapsed Catholic.
– Teach me in French, like she would have said it.
He understands.
– Good for my memory, he jokes.

– Je veux Salut Marie,
pleine de grâce

we begin

– le Seigneur est avec vous.
Vous êtes bénie entre toutes
les femmes et Jésus,
le fruit de vos entrailles, est béni.

Mary, yes, I will pray to Mary now
Mother Mary come to me

such comfort in the ancient story
of a mother who loved
a mother who lost
her son

mine sure wasn't Jesus
but oh how he suffered

Ordinary did she say ordinary
no moving no laughing no crying
a chorus from childhood

no obituary
    obituary
no moving no laughing no crying

obituary
no moving no laughing no crying

    one word
    delivers
    a complete body blow
        obituary
a word punch
    right to the solar plexus

    Instead of hitting back
    I stick out my tongue
    give the raspberry
    instead of hitting
    come as close
    to spitting on anyone
    as I ever have
    but oh how
    I want to hit
        something
someone

If I had a hammer

I'd shatter the stained glass window
of daylight

kick the moon out of the sky

then grow knives for fingernails

I need to claw something until it bleeds

Finally yes here you are
my oldest son
you
who loved
could not save
your little brother
big brother
little father
that you were
when you were children
when it seemed so long too long
it was three of us
against the world
My son my man son
how I loved
being a mother of little boys
but I have
never learned
how to be the mother of men
but here you are
we are, my son
yes we will weep
in each other's arms
but we two
too wounded
to comfort each other
yes an end
to his suffering
yes, to his
but not ours
oh my son
with those
melting
chocolate brown eyes
what if
the seventeen
year old I was
had never said yes
to you?

Death-struck dumb

melting into numbness

such strange space
ah yes, death yields
a temporary trust new-found astounding intimacy

for us all

these moments

hold gifts
heal rifts

crack the shell of any heart

we know a hidden sacred secret:
no matter how messy the past the present
it will get messier
yet for now
see how
all is forgiven
how any darkness shrivels to the size of a pea
there is only overwhelming LOVE
how is it family and friends
no matter what mattered yesterday
now greet to gather each other up
proof of larger truths
of life and love
how we hug
how we hold
how we wrap our arms around each other
the only storage space
we
ever
really
need

1:33 A.M. on March 4

I write

my son's full name

followed by dates

November 18, 1980 – March 2, 2018

Why is it when I write or read

things become most real to me

No mother should ever have to write her child's obituary

Not everything can be written down. Not this.
Not everything can be re-written. Not this.

My heart's been drilled out of my chest.
I need a rag to stuff in its place
stop the bleeding
maybe an old terrycloth towel shoved in a gas tank
desperate people use when they've lost the cap

– how are you doing, we keep asking each other

How to describe not breathing but living?

        being buried alive

right now at ***this moment*** I know this:

I need emergency scuba gear
self-contained underground breathing apparatus
I'm thinking of those men who tried recovering dead bodies
from the Westray Mine disaster
oxygen packs on their backs like wings
as they went into the treacherous shafts

angels of the underground

all our years of rescue attempts

      and then, after that, just hope…

        all of that…over.

Yet that is what I need – an air pack

           so I can breathe here underground

when we go, tomorrow, to recover his body.

They tell me I cannot touch him
seriously?
of course I do
kiss and kiss and kiss
his wax-like forehead touch his chest
where his heart no longer beats

    who dressed him?
    he should be wearing red,
    his favourite colour,
    or turquoise blue

    his lips are drawn

    too thin

    too sad

    how I wanted to needed to see him

but now...

I cannot un-see

    tell me how does any mother live in the world

        after having seen their child

    lifeless?

Tell me, Jesus Christ.

Can you tell me that?

How did your mother feel?

TELL me Tell me…will someone tell me
how to live turned inside out?

JANGLED nerves

D
    A
       N
          G
            L
               $^I N_G$

Skin outside in   raw as a burn victim   all has slipped sideways
                                         a dizziness
spinning eyes rolling all the way round becoming small ball
                              bearings in a game of pinball
inside my skull

is that cranium – milky white brain stuff – coils of a labyrinth?

FUCK
it's so dark in here.

       Yes, I said FUCK

Trillions and trillions of times FUCK if there was ever a fucking
time to say fuck it would be fucking now

Now a Mary named Marie – she feeds us
                                she gives us a bed
                                she wraps us in blankets and love

together they tether us here so I don't float away like some helium
human, though I'm ready to burst. And they talk to us softly, she
weeps with me often, the softest of eyes they are here helping
Gilles to be not so alone with the moaning the groaning insane
creature beside him one night I think we drink too much but I
can't remember but drunk is not good besides there's not enough
wine to numb me enough and I'm so cold all the time. Marie offers
me scarves to wear because all black is too black is too black and
besides she's not letting me go out there all alone her scarf is her
arm still around me even if she's not there then she finds a picture
from years back of Dee with his arms around me hugging me so
tight as if smothering his mother with love all you see is the top
of my hat and a fringe of my hair. The look on his face is so full of
love and there I am tucked in his arms, her arms, and she is a friend
I will never be able to thank, a mother Mary to me, an angel, who
gives me the gift of remembering the hugs of my son.

Biblical themes

in umbilical dreams

giant lima bean

babies

floating outside

empty amniotic

sacs

astronauts

trying to get back

to the mother ship

– Oma Oma Oma

– Grandson!

all the way here
from British Columbia
he cups my chin in his hands
his touch the zap!
of an electric shock
topaz tiger's eyes
calming me

– Oma, Daddy was a good soul!
– Yes, he was
is is is is is is

Grandson, how do you know this word – soul?

Your memorial service is on a storm day. Full circle, baby. Life cycle. You, six weeks early, almost born in a snowbank, first storm of the year that year. I can still replay that trip moment by moment,

zig

        zag   .

of

             cars

slid sideways

       p
all the way u

York Street

me doubled over so low I'm eye to eye with the silver button of the glove compartment, poking out like my belly button focal point focal point find the fuck the focal point the pain – so terrified you were coming, but your father plowed through in that emerald green CJ5 Jeep of ours and we made it to the hospital just in time – well, you know that part of the story. I've told you so many times.

But you don't know this part, the part where I've always thought where did they take you why did it take so long to hear you cry, but then I heard you and they brought you back and then you on my belly craning your neck turning your face to mine opening those black bean eyes just slits at first squinting then wider and wider blinking at brightness but finding me, holding my gaze as if dazed so amazed there you are hey there hiya, Mama, then you began to suckle and coo.

Only I know that part, how you looked in my eyes: how much love at first sight. Or do you, tell me, is that memory of birth and love something that stays with you beyond your death?

For love never dies for the living
Tell me, please
tell me
that love never dies for the dead.

He said he really only knew your shiny side

there he is singing, yes, there is your childhood friend
singing a song called

"Precious Memories"

    people are leaving

why are they leaving

    before the song is over?

– come back come back come back don't go

A precious memory:
    you two racing through that
little yellow crooked house
on Charlotte Street
your laughter
the sound of the sun in May

In the pantry, I touch a container
of protein powder
zap! powered back
here we are
mother and son
in the grocery aisle
together
his voice, his laugh
comparing brands and prices
next to the pharmacy aisle
his methadone zone

he was trying
trying so hard
to get healthy

right there in the pantry
I've discovered
some kind of time travel

my legs disappear
I'm on the floor

Until G comes to gather me up

I am learning

there's a difference between a flashback and memory

memory is a remembering…

flashback

a dis-member-ing

crying
this much
gives a person
an ice cream headache

Once,

When I was a mother of babies
I rocked them
made things better
When I was a mother of toddlers
I helped them with whatever
When I was a mother of teens
I prayed when they went wild
Now I am a mother of adults
Helpless as a child.

Now?

Now I am a mother
who has lost a child
there's no name for me
so call me wild.
I am a wild mother
a feral mother
wild with love
sorrow
rage
pain

I am the wild spitting wind
I am love's hurricane

Now I am a mother
who has lost a son
there's no name for me
so just call me

Undone.

– I can't imagine, people keep saying

– No, you can't. And trust me. You don't want to.

Ever.

The only time you will ever hear me say

failure of imagination is a blessing

I take a vase of purple orchids from the table at the church reception.
This bouquet, from our family. Someone tells me no, to leave it.

Mine! I snap, **mine!**

I hold the orchids in my lap for two hours on the drive home.
So fragile, beautiful.

I hold the purple flowers in my lap as if they are a baby.

There are thirty-seven orchids blooming – a coincidence, perhaps.
One for every year of your life, my son.

I come from a long line of women who have lost their sons

two aunts, a great-grandmother, a grandmother, my mother

Sometimes I picture all of us ululating arms around each other's
waists shuffle-bumping in a strange ceremonial conga line a dance
against despair we could bring the world to its knees if you listen
to what we sing we are the fierce force field we speak code we
sometimes sing in a chorus in Janis Joplin's voice

nothing left to lose

My initiation has just begun

Home for a visit once, just after my brother died, I notice
tucked into the side of the bathroom mirror, a small piece of paper
with my mother's handwriting on it. I lean forward, read

You won't always be this sad

So I picture my mother washing her face each morning
looking at herself
trying trying trying to tell herself this sadness would get better

Now

my mother
holds me in her arms,
my best friend in this new pain

– remember what I wrote, she whispers or do I imagine this
– you won't always be this sad, she whispers or do I imagine this
– softer, she tells me
– the pain will get "softer," yes she tell me this

seconds moments hours days pass

five days my mother and sisters stay
then leave
as if they were never here

except I hear her whisper

you won't always be this sad

I write the note out for myself

You won't always be this sad

tuck it in my bathroom mirror

but it does no good right now

I've avoided the mirror

for fear of being spooked

Last week
no reflection
that resembled anyone
I recognized
looked back at me

Yesterday, I swear,
there was no reflection at all.

Today, I am not grateful
Today, I can't forgive
I don't want to kill myself
I just don't want to live

Jesus

was

        my imaginary playmate when I was a child

I used to make him turn his back
when I was putting on my pajamas

        He moved away when I was around ten

Now, finding myself in times of trouble, he's back…sort of

still doesn't talk much

But Mother Mary and Paul McCartney?

Now they are quite the duo

        my new imaginary playmates.

Speaking words of wisdom
Let it be
Let it be let it be…how can I let it be?

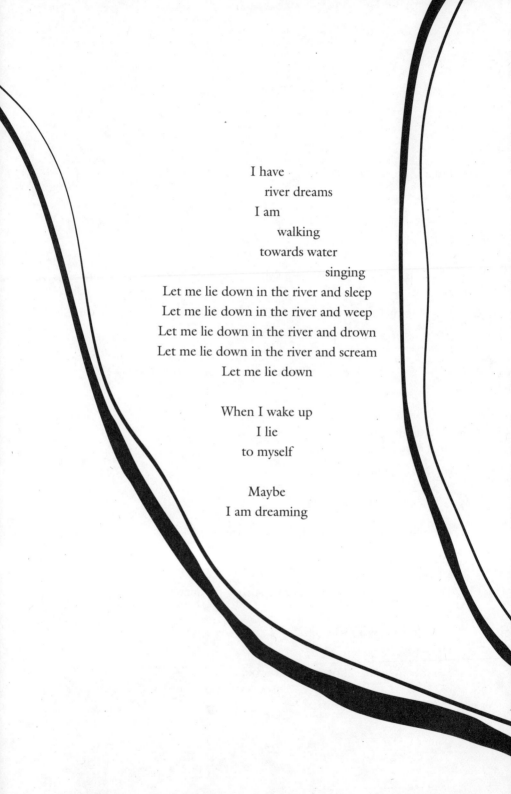

I have
river dreams
I am
walking
towards water
singing
Let me lie down in the river and sleep
Let me lie down in the river and weep
Let me lie down in the river and drown
Let me lie down in the river and scream
Let me lie down

When I wake up
I lie
to myself

Maybe
I am dreaming

Everything's too loud

too fast

too bright

so
this is the unrelenting pain
called sorrow

I know
I will be just as sad
as mad

tomorrow

how do I live with not knowing?

how did he die? How?

months they said before the autopsy report

when we will know how

if not why

crying	waking up	crying
crying	going to sleep	crying
crying	all day long day in day out snot bawl	crying
crying	running up the dirt road	crying
crying	curled up in a ball on the floor	crying
crying	drunk in the parked car	crying
crying	barefoot in the snow	crying
crying	choking in each other's arms	crying
crying	on the phone to his brother	crying
crying	wailing screaming by the ocean	crying
crying	reading every card	crying
crying	because of kindness	crying
crying	because of beauty	crying
crying	because I'm tired of crying	crying
crying	to the dog	crying
crying	telling the horses why I'm crying	crying
crying	in the tub	crying
crying	in the shower	crying
crying	on the spin bike	crying
crying	in the gym class	crying
crying	in the dollar store	crying
crying	listening to music	crying
crying	looking at baby pictures	crying
crying	wearing his clothes	crying
crying	smelling his shampoo	crying
crying	standing where he hugged me	crying
crying	kissing his pictures	crying
crying	trying to read a book	crying
crying	doing the laundry	crying
crying	trying to breathe	crying

but death has taken my breath

enough
enough

but it is only the beginning

Our family lived on a street
behind the Moncton City Hospital
each night before I settled down
I had this ritual: I would kneel on my bed
press my face against the window, the
screen in summer the frosted pane in winter,
turn my head so I could see
the side of the hospital facing us.

In every window every topaz square of light
I imagined someone in pain or dying
so would breathe a prayer
– Get better soon!
– Jesus, please make all the sick and dying
people all better.

I did this from the age of four until I was twelve
on a fairly regular basis
never realizing until many years later
I was practicing a form of tonglen
taught to me by a Buddhist therapist
who may have saved my life
when she taught me to breathe
that I could beam to others for others

Ah, bodhisattva
Ah, bodhicitta

Now I struggle for my own breath
stare out the bedroom window
where the moon's light
takes the shape of crucifix
bludgeons me
as it enters my chest

I pray for myself
Jesus Mary Tara
healing gods
angels of Divine Being Bhuddha
whoever
I am dying

please please please
take away this pain
or let me die

energy washes
through me
emerges from the cold black window

I sense the presence of a friend
who died a few years back

I'm so very glad to see her

She comes to me, strokes my cheek,
whispers, there there there there
until I stop shuddering and breathe and fall asleep

I've heard of those dreams where someone who's died pays you a visit, makes a brief appearance, gives you a message. I've had a few before now but I've not told many for fear of sounding crazy or pathetic or unintelligent or irreverent or silly, like those people who pay money to mediums to read their astrological charts to channel the dead as if the summoning of spirits is a parlour game, a fun thing to do one day with girlfriends, a lark.

Okay, I confess. I've done that, too. And taken it seriously.

After all, admitting one can talk to the dead, or worse, the dead can talk to you, is, some say, the last taboo, a forbidden thing of which we must not speak or utter to another.

No we must keep this to ourselves or perhaps the page. Or whatever god one chooses.

Perhaps it's the moon we confide in – what else to do when you are split wide open by the sword of night?

But

there are those of us – and we usually know each other when we meet – who have always known the world of spirits who have always talked to spirits and heard them talk amongst themselves; most children do this until a certain age, they call it night terrors they call it overactive imagination, imaginary playmates – make no mistake, children live in a thin place still half-submerged in the world they came from, still in close contact with the invisible ones or sometimes replaying a time in a former life as if it were a movie. Well, it could be so – who knows for sure what happens in inner space?

Inner space
inner space
so many galaxies there
to explore

endless, really.

So tell me, have you ever had a visitation
from the dead
a message in a dream
the ticklish touch of a spirit passing by?

Have you ever really listened to the music of the wind
as you begged please please please

I just need to see you one more time again?

We are in an airport waiting at the arrivals gate. Dee is coming,
     coming home.
There are plate glass windows shot through with white light so
     bright it hurts our eyes
so we have to squint to see. G's hand on my shoulder. Yes, we are
     in an airport
waiting at the arrivals gate excited because Dee is coming home!
We know we'll see him any minute – then there he is!

He is four not thirty-seven, my happy boy the joy he was before he
     went into a world
that stopped his music and bruised his glad heart I run towards him,
kneel down, hug squeeze kiss his cheeks

– mama, I never want to go that far away for that long ever again

– but you never have to

Duct taped to the side of his snowsuit are two vinyl records, LPs

– what's this honey? What's this for?

A sheepish grin

– well you know, Mama, how I'm always losing things?

Before I can answer him, he looks at me seriously

– because you know, Mama, you can't lose the music

gone he is gone when I open my eyes I am standing at my
bedroom window exhaling see my breath upon the windowpane

Is it possible for a person to hold their breath for eight days?

You can't lose the music

because you know, Mama, you can't lose the music

This is code.
I will discover what this means.

One night when I was five
            my father found me crying
Is there a God, I asked?
            How do I know God is real
If I can't see GOD?
Wordless, my father lifted me
            from quilts to window ledge
For an answer,
            pointed to the stars.

Once upon a time this was
            answer enough

But tonight

            barefoot in the snow
I am screaming at the stars
                        like an unholy fool

      pinpricks of light streaming down

like some kind of joke   because
            God's not
and those stars are deathly cold, indifferent, cruel

Days are not days
for time is not time
you know that now
for even now is a wisp
a feather a breath
a nothing you cannot
hold onto
a whirlpool of smoke
of murmuring memories
coming at you at the speed of light
a surround sound video
playing inside your head
you want to turn off
(but you don't want to turn off)
time is not time
you know that now
time is not time
never has been
never will be
such a thing as life Time
or dead line
days are not days
you live second by breath
by breath

I

see things
                    monstrous things

crawling things

                            skeleton hands

grabbing out for my neck

in the darkness

I keep tumbling
down
down
down

At the very bottom

something grotesque

                    I can't quite discriminate

but yes

in the heart of darkness the horror horror

but how the greatest horror is seeing

how right beside it

lies the beauty the beauty

so this is a truth I glimpsed:
side by side
they coincide
they co-exist joy sorrow good evil
life death

all dualities c
                  o   l   l a p se   into a complex oneness

when I had no place to go

except to stare death in the face

LOVE lifted me

      back to the surface

some days it feels like I am living at the edge

on the lip of a Grand Canyon–sized gap

but that's when

                LOVE gives me a parachute

so my next tumble down

the landing is smoother

I arrive in a different place

Somehow, always

I see Mary's face

Who knew?

Hers is the face of all mothers who mourn
Hers are the arms where LOVE was and is and ever is born

Divine Feminine

Mother of shimmering

Stardust Goddess

I live in a thin place now

    A threshold place

        between

                the realms of the living and the dead

        for here is where I might see him

there! Up on the hill

in that place where he wanted to build his home

      or around the corner

            running into my arms

or maybe, yes, I will hear him laugh

       or call: Mama Mama Mama

     and I can hold him again while he cries

        so yes…I must set up camp

            here in this thin place

make a fire

     send him smoke signals'

        so he knows

I am waiting

RECEIVING

You wouldn't believe what once or
twice I have seen. I'll just
tell you this:
only if there are angels in your head will you
ever, possibly, see one.

— MARY OLIVER

I open my eyes
only to find out
everything has melted to a liquid gold
I am blinded by
light

So what can I do
with this knowledge of angels
except fall to my knees
and
sing?

Nothing's as welcome as spring after an endless winter
we are still waiting watching
potholes swallow wheels of cars
bump-thumping loud
the sound the grind and thrash

Where is all the juice and joy – dirt rise up!
we long for mudslush rush of river
still glazed over beneath skies
the soft grey like daze of pussywillows:
christ lord, the monochromatic is monotonous
this is an invocation:
bring on the green
the glory
dream dramatic
hark lark harbinger
on the back of the nuthatch spring
take wing!

Good god, a gold morning
the sun is out
oh chickadees!
I give thanks
for days like these

Week five
I wake up
sunlight splashing around me

– THE SUN! Finally.

– Don't you think it strange, I ask
how ever since he died
the sun hasn't shone until today?

It is as if I have startled
my love of so many years
he looks at me
as if he might be afraid
his face a mixture:
compassion, relief.

– But it has, he says gently,
the sun's been out before today

– No, I say, not until today
but even as I protest
I realize this can't be so.

but the moon the moon
every night the moon
so bright
I'd squint my eyes
until the beams
·became a crucifix

How curious
mysterious

I've lived five weeks
in a pre-dawn darkness
temporarily blind to sunlight
the stars, just holes in the sky

yet the moon never left

LOVE still burning bright

Yes, somewhere deep inside
darkness held me
like a friend
let me hide
until today

so I dip my hands
in that splash of sun
wash my face
awake
in joy and wonder

Yesterday when the river opened
so did my heart
flowing water swirled a reminder
how constant change
how living is an art
This river is a Goddess
she quenches thirst
she fills smalls pools with sacred visions
(just weeks ago she held my screams
and carried them out to sea)
She offers me
occasional prayers

Her name is Mother Mary
Her name is Eleos
Her name is Kuan Yin
Her name is Tara
Her name is Mercy
Her name is Dolores

Her name is Catherine
Her name is Cindy
Her name is Dawn
Her name is Theresa
Her name is Gayle
Her name is Paula
Her name is Barbara
Her name is Jean

Her name is yours
Her name is mine.

She writes

I dreamt of you last night, I visited you at your home and you just
fell into my arms, and stayed by my side, and cried and cried and
cried. we must have come together in our dreams. I am holding
you up and holding your heart in the palm of my hands
while you are struggling to survive.

Put some tobacco out today and offer it to the earth.
if you don't have that, then use sage, cedar, or sweetgrass, or all.
Just thank the creator for having the time you did with your son.
he will always be with you, you can never lose him as he is now
back inside of you, in your heart. you carry his essence, his spirit.
There is no right or wrong, there is no, if onlys and what ifs, there
is only love, and that you both had for each other.
that is where you will find your peace with yourself and together
with him.

Tears are sacred, they come from our wombs that we carried our
children in, that nurtured them and kept them safe, remember
that the sacred water we cry comes not only from our womb, but
is connected all the way back to our very first grandmother and
she is with you today, all your grandmothers are with you today I
know that.
that is how we stand up and walk through this time.
praying for you.
i will see you today my dear friend.
msit no'kmaq all my relations

He writes

I've really been wanting to say something, but really been uncertain what to say. Of all the standard phrases I've heard the best is in Finnish:

"Otan osaa suruasi,"

which means "Let me carry a small piece of your pain."

"Let me" because it is our glad responsibility, as a community, to share in these things.

"Small" because of course it is the one who loses someone who has to bear so much.

In searching for snippets of wisdom I also found this from the source:

"There is a world within this one where you can go and come undone and when your tears have stopped a while a small sun shines its warm heart smile."

Beautiful eh? Another of many wise words you've put out there for us, which is why so many are willing to share your pain.

She writes

You will be whole again, I promise you

And she, who has also lost a son, who only ever met me once,
sends me a quilt she stitched when she heard of Dee's death and so
I weep with gladness because she knows *she knows* I am in pieces,
she knows, she knows, and she *promises* me and so many nights
when it gets too unbearable I wrap this quilt around me and I rock
and believe, I believe, the pain will get softer and I hear my mother
whisper *you won't always be this sad* and then

one night in the dark I am brave begin to nibble the
Peppermint Pattie my neighbour delivered – o love thy neighbour
is easy when thy neighbour is easy to love – down goes that
sweetness past the lump in my throat, yes I swallow it down feel its
kiss in my belly now a piece of mandarin orange –

there, wrapped in that quilt for the first time in weeks

there is taste

burst of flavour

tang on my tongue

The smell of oranges, someone once told me, means angels are
close by.

I only know this: two more Marys have delivered me.

Every bird's an angel
every tree a soul
who's travelled here a while
then journeyed on.

Grief cracks open
hidden selves
when I am brave enough
to look inside
when I am still enough
to listen to the wisdom
deep sorrow offers

I say thank you
thank you thank you

as I hear the voices of the dead

forever after

feel spirits
and Spirit
guiding us along

LOVE whispers
I am by your side
I am I am
Fear not.

Thank you
for the air!
Here's to the kind of day the air is gulp-able
feels like you just bit into an apple: crisp, delicious.
Here's to a juicy day. A juicy life. The air.
A day you feel
apple juice dripping
down
your
chin.

Such beauty

exists in the midst

of sorrow's mist

and

broken-openness

such clarity

in despair

such music here

in silence

I saw an angel on the hill today in the place where he wanted
to build his house. He brought me there last fall to show me
and when we got there the wind was blowing he said look and
I said wow and he said I see everything the whole pasture the
animals this is the view I want so I saw him up there today I was
sitting underneath the apple tree and I looked up and there was
a shimmering like a tall tall shadow of tinfoil glimmering and I
thought oh it must be a trick of light and so I stood up and it
moved and it moved again and I walked a few paces and it moved
again but it didn't really go it didn't go away yes that I saw on the
hill today

For ye shall go out with joy, and be led forth with peace; the
mountains and the hills shall break forth before you into singing,
and all the trees of the field shall clap their hands.

— ISAIAH, 55:12

Sorry, Isaiah, now I read and read you, Isaiah

but still it's more like I go out with weeping

led forth by anguish

the mountains and hills

are solid   too high   silent

the bare-branched trees of the field

have no leafy hands to wave or clap

instead, they rattle – skeleton bones

in the wind.

listening now in this silence

there is a faint and distant song

perhaps one day I will hear

       singing

that for now only the trees

          the river gods

applaud

I know I will not find

what I'm seeking

in books or words

but I keep reading

words and study

distract me

the brain is an ally at times

yes, even a fractured brain offers time out

I still find it strange how I "knew" at once, knew I would need new language, new words to comfort me, new rituals, knew I would need Mother Mary now and until the hour of my death.

So maybe my grand-mère and ma belle mère, those good Catholic childbearing madonnas swooped down from the heavens those first hours. Winged women.
Guardian angels. Spirits. Maybe.

Sometimes, I still think I feel the air stir as if someone is there.
I can imagine their wings, fanning me.
Or maybe, billows for my lungs when I cannot breathe.

So go chasing Mary
like some new game of Trivial Pursuit
no call it Survival Pursuit
when in real Jeopardy

do do do do do do do do do do do do dodododo

Theology for a thousand
The study or doctrine relating to the Virgin Mary.
What is Mariology
Correct, for 1,000!
Fact: The first known use of the word "Mariology" was in 1857
Yes, you would be a mariologist if you were versed in Mariology
Can you use the adjective Mariological in a sentence?

After her son's death she developed a Mariological obsession
Sometimes she stared at Boticelli's Madonnas for hours

Oh, and so many names she goes by
Mother of Jesus.
I'm not swearing. Then there's
Blessed Mother, Our Lady, Queen of Heaven
The epithets
Star of the sea, Queen of heaven, Cause of our joy,
The invocations
Theotokos Panagia
Mother of Mercy
Our Lady of Guadalupe

Mary
Also Slam-Banger of Pots and Pans
Hurler of Teacups
Wild Drummer of Djembe songs
Mad Runner on Dirt Roads
Silent Screamer Behind that Mona Lisa Smile
Whisperer of Lullabies
Collector of Tears

I know Mary as all the

GRAND MOTHERS

the ones who live beyond life
come to us
in the hours of need

small wonder I want to stay inside
sip green tea with my Marys
hear them whisper *you won't always be this sad*

but I know I must keep going out

keep going forth

because I can't lose the music

or at least the possibility

So Mary and I go out dancing with Tara
all the colours of Tara
green Tara white Tara
we dance with scarves
we chant a sweet chorus
we dance!

perhaps I will offer my self in sun salutations again one day

for now we pray
as we sway with our bodies

om tare tuttare ture soha

yes, we chant and dance

om tare tuttare ture soha

now I dance through the labyrinth, singing,

om tare tuttare ture soha

no, we shall NOT lose the music

om tare tuttare ture soha

Dear Mary Oliver,

This morning three flocks
    of wild geese flew over the river
        so close to the house
            when we stepped out
                we could hear the thrumming
                    of their wings
                                and of course, I thought of you
                                    thought of that first line
                                of your poem, telling us
                            we do not have to be good
                        yes, and I say

we have to fill in our own blanks.
We do not have to be sad
or present
or anxious
or joyful
or quiet
well, I could go on...
except
I do have to be grateful
and the sun is shining
I need to go out
to follow my imaginings
perhaps fly for a bit
with those
wild, wild geese.

Everyone's a poet

Yes, don't you see

real poets hide inside everyone
real poets don't always
write in lines or words

but they might build a house
like my Gilles did
or create a space for silence
show up and listen
like my friend Rita does
or plant gardens
like Dee did
before he died .

real poets hide
in space
stars
beams
blooms

Don't you see I want to shout out to anyone who will listen *I need
you to see   to know
to know this*

everyone's a poet

every soul

a poem

don't you see? you need to see

I step outside
for the first time in a long time
or maybe it is the first time
I want to step outside
the air is fresh
as a glass of water
I am surrounded
                                        by all these yellow butterflies
hundreds really hundreds
flying from the trees
as if they'd just emerged from a cocoon
as if they were saying
yes look
we are still here with you
we who you loved
who you think are gone
look see us when we greet you

Bless all the yellow butterflies
Bless the bottle blue silver wings
                                        of dragonflies

        Bless the birds, the crows, the wrens
            Bless us children, women, men.

Angels in the faces of those I meet
especially in children, in animals
I hear them, too
singing in trees when the leaves rustle.

Or that clack of pebbles
at the edge of the ocean
when waves come in
slide over those speckled round rocks
and then recede...

Yes so easy to picture
rock-clacking
mermaid castanets
as uproarious
glorious laughter of gods.

One night,
the sound of mandolins cymbals tin flutes
maybe harps woke me up
led me to a window where
there was no parade passing by
only the moon smiled down.

Yet I hear such things sometimes
think if only I could catch that beauty
let others hear what I hear
we'd all be swooning with love bursting
crying out how can anything here on this sad earth
be so achingly beautiful?

I am crazy with love
It doesn't matter.

I know
it **really** doesn't anymore.

Besides, my children always reassured me:

*Mama, you're a good kind
of crazy.*

On yesterday's beach walk
marram grass was golden
sand as tanned as leather
the ocean curled a muddy lip
against this hostile weather.

Barefoot beneath a sky
a dark metallic grey
I found a heart of stone
that melted mine
for a moment –
washed this pain away.

My grandson asks is this Dad's shampoo

I say yes and so we anoint ourselves

pouring

on

the smells

the way we pull his shirts

over our heads

the way I wear his coat

so when I hug his children

they will feel his arms around them

so that I feel his arms around me

The distance – and the difference – between us dwindled and vanished. We could meet, mingle, and blend. Neither one of us existed any more; for a time there was a single being that was both."

— JOHN WYNDHAM, *The Chrysalids*

So. This is a true story.
This is a story that happened to me.
Not an aunt or a friend. To me.

I was eighteen when I was given proof that thoughts could travel. I'd known this was true long before, seemed something I always knew and thought everyone did but no one spoke of. Kind of like masturbation. I thought this way right up until we had to read the novel *The Chrysalids* in high school. I was startled because everyone seemed to think mind communication was a radical concept. How could I explain I'd been doing some form of this all my life?

So the story goes like this: my baby was only a few months old when I got sick one night, waking up shortly before midnight. I was violently ill. It was the first time I'd been sick without my mother. I retched and cried and called out for my mother all night long until about four, when the waves stopped and I crawled back to bed. I went to sleep, praying the baby would sleep past his usual five o'clock wake time. He slept until around seven thirty.

It was a Saturday morning and my husband had left early to go on a camping trip. I knew I was too weak and still sick and would need help that day.

I called my mother at about nine. Before I blubbered out my problems, I mumbled the usual greeting.

Hi Mom, how are you today?

Not very well, she said, hardly slept a wink. It was the darndest thing. I woke up around midnight thinking I heard somebody being sick. Heard the toilet flush, heard someone calling for me. I woke your father up and he went and checked downstairs. The kids were sound asleep. He said, it's just a dream, and went back to sleep. But it kept up. All night long. Until around four. It was so real. I tell you. It wasn't a dream.

I stared at the phone and finally said, It was me, Mum. I woke up, was sick, went back to bed around four.

My mother didn't miss a beat:

I knew it!

She covered the mouthpiece and called to my father: Ken, I told you it was real. It was.... As she said my name, her voice trailed off as we both realized the enormity of what we were actually saying. We lived miles away from one another...but I had reached her. With exact timing.

This became something of a family legend. My dad quipping, Well your name rhymes with *witch* after all – hahaha – always knew it! The two of you.

The thing is we accepted this story and I tucked it away to an extent. Life goes on. I often had dreams that came true and sensed things before they happened. There was that real spooky time in a store where a baby in a stroller reached out her arms to me and said *Mama Mama Mama* and her mother and father looked at me strangely and she kept it up and her mother said she's not your mother and they quickly scooted her away. I read a lot of Edgar Cayce.

But always, this story of my mother and me, now part of our family legend, is what convinced me our thoughts have the power to travel.

You cannot call this a "coincidence."

Oh yes, how waves of sound can carry things. Imagine the wind curling around uttered words, a soft cyclone of smoke whirling from here to there. Me to you. Worlds to worlds.

Oh how mothers hear their children.

This is why I hear her every day now, saying,
you won't always be this sad.

This is why I believe that we have not even begun to tap into the extraordinary powers we have in the galaxies of inner space.

This is why I know my son still speaks to me, and I to him.

This is why I believe Dee when he told me he was not alone the moment he died but that I was with him when he died.

This is why I have a dog. Oscar the dog told me.

This is why I believe in all I do not know but know.

This is why I have faith in love, travelling.

That we can breathe our thoughts and hopes and dreams and prayers through air and wind and space and over times long gone.

See, I have proof. There, I've said it.

Not that I ever really needed proof to have faith.

But most days, this is the story and knowledge and experience that keeps me tethered here.

And of course, my dog. The dog whose eyes Dee told me to look into, and when I did I would see his love for me.

I have faith in dogs. Dogs are gods are dogs are gods.

Oh, I have faith.

I have faith in dreams and Bugs Bunny and beauty.

This happens:
I wake up one morning...laughing
I dreamt Elmer Fudd was giving the weather report

– Hewo folks! No wabbbits today but it's going to be a weawy,
weawy, weawy sunny day

I'm laughing not crying and look out the window

– oh honey, I woke up laughing not crying and look look I have
such a beautiful place to be sad in!

I start crying

and he says what

and I say

I have such a beautiful place to be sad in, look at that river,
sparkling, I mean I could be this sad and in a refugee camp or think
of my friend Marie up north who lost three children and it's so
cold there or a basement apartment with rats!

Elmer Fudd gave me the weather report in a dream and I woke up
laughing and have a beautiful place to be sad in

and he says

– so stop crying then honey and go write that down
A beautiful place to be sad in. That's a good one.

That day you wake up laughing
is the beginning of the beginning again

you don't have to count your blessings
when you know you are blessed
blessed
by beauty
wherever you look
wherever you are

whoever you are
keep looking deep enough searching far enough
until you have a dream
to wake you up laughing

may all beings find
a beautiful place to be sad in

those who are on the other side

are never very

far

away

they are

ever there

over there

waving

saying we're fine just fine

another day is done
I have lived to see and hear its nowness
felt the light
watched an eagle
picked up a letter
read loving words
walked bearing unbearable sadness
yet still glimpsed beauty gave thanks
but there is still the long dark night ahead where my only comfort
is moon songs listen I try to listen in silence but still I cannot
breathe in this quicksand of grief

Last night stars fell from the sky
now in the frosted fields, they lie
such glitter dazzle blinding bright
each step you take, you fill with light
lovers and fools we humans are
perhaps each soul
a hidden star
a galaxy on earth to find
in undiscovered fields of shine.

Solvitur ambulando

– DIOGENES

Walk.

Okay, that I can do, have been doing, will do.
One step at a time.
Is there any other way to walk?
On water.
Very funny. I walk. In the labyrinth. Even in winter.
Walk on.

RETURNING

There is the music of Heaven in all things.

— HILDEGARD OF BINGEN

There is nothing like death to make you wonder what you have faith in. Or don't.

I have faith in dogs because dogs are gods are dogs.

Go back to your own faith tradition and go deeper said the Dalai Lama to thousands of us in the convention centre in Washington DC. This was 2003.

Faith tradition. Not religion.

I went deeper. Or thought I did. I found Centering Prayer. I found the Beguines. Women of old who loved God and community and were often burned at the stake.

But deeper, really deeper, there is the piercing of beauty and love.

I think I know now what Blake meant – to "bear the beams of love."

When I was a child I used to reach out my hand thinking the
darkness was furry and I could stroke the air and it would feel
like my mother's racoon coat I used to bury my face in whenever
I went hiding in the front hall closet in a game of hide-and-seek.
Or sometimes I went to hide there when I just wanted to still
everything. Get away from the noise of the television and everyone.

I do not want to return. It is too noisy and fast.
There must be some way to re-enter what some call reality.

In morning meditation I receive a pine cone from some hooded creature who reminds me a bit of Darth Vader. Pine cone? I'm curious...so I google and I get *Pine*, the tree, comes from the Latin *pinus*, which is related to an earlier Indo-European word meaning "resin" or "sap," which pine trees possess in abundance. *Pine*, the act of mooning about in the wake of lost love, comes from the Latin *poena*, meaning "punishment," which also gave us "pain" and "penalty." So, right, like it's all connected to some kind of third-eye powerful spirit stuff

I like this. It's a message, right? A signal, a clue.

Pine cone follow the pine cone a way out of pain pine pain

I keep thinking repeating chiming rhyming

Pine how about wine no

pine cone pine cone until finally I hear

cone of pining

That's it!

A cone of pining

A cone of pining?

Like a cone of silence

Yes, I am learning now

how to come and go from there

I'm going to the Superstore in a stupor

stupor store – ha ha I'm a riot

I choose a Superstore an hour away
where no one will know me

get out of the car
get halfway to the entrance
run back to the car

maybe you saw me
with my head on the steering wheel

maybe you saw me
trying to breathe

maybe you saw me
driving the roads
maybe you saw that wild woman
behind the windshield
with the contorted face

oh how many of us wailing ones
are driving
around in cars

because

we can scream and scream and scream

inside a safety dome

inside a cone of pining

– it's okay, says my mother
say, good job I got that far
next time you will get to the door
go in, get through the aisles
all the way to the cash
you will buy groceries again

next try
I get in
find it hard to focus in the aisles
especially near the pharmacy section

I'm saying underneath my breath as I put in my debit card

I did it I did it

then there is a tap on my shoulder

the cashier behind me

I know her and she says
– I am so sorry for your loss

and she holds me and we weep and I say, I just got groceries for
the first time

maybe you saw her?

the brave brave woman who knew how much I needed a hug

the one not afraid to weep in front of her customers.

I think of her often

for I think yes, that is what we need

a world of people reaching out , no matter what

damn the protocol

saying I love you I love you I love you

remembering it will never be business as usual

and me forgiving

        over and over

            those who forget

      or simply cannot face this wild unravelling

Real-world functioning time:
After midnight in a one-star hotel
in a distant city. Room's clean but I run a bath
fill it with lavender slide underneath the sheets
throw back the fake velour bedspread I try not to touch.

I'm reading my keynote for tomorrow but now someone's arrived
next door. Walls, paper thin. The man starts coughing, choking on
his phlegm so loud as if he's lying on the pillow right next to me
and I think, gross, phleghm, germs, insomnia, please dear God will
I have to listen to this all night?

I keep reading.

He stops coughing suddenly
heaves a deep sigh
so I think dear lord he's croaked
should I call the front desk – until, after a minute or so

a different sound

I realize he is crying
he cries and cries as if
UP UNTIL NOW
he's been holding in
an entire lifetime of pain

I get it.

just last week there was that day
a day I realized it wasn't only Dee's death
I was grieving

it was the life he never had
it was all the times I hadn't cried
all the times to come
all the pain of men like this
all the pain of women
all the pain in this jeezlus fucked up beautiful sad world

For a second, I pictured myself putting my hands
on the locked door adjoining our two rooms
whispering to the wall, sir, sir, please do not cry
talk to me instead

you can tell me your sorrow
I know about sorrow
or, shh now,
sir, let me tell you a poem
a lullaby about a moon
how you will be with people
you love forever and after

or mister, I know what you need
Dog. Dog. You need to find Dog
because Dog will love you

or mister just switch the channel in your head
or mister put your hand on the door
and we will trace the design of a labyrinth
together.

But of course, I do nothing.

I sit there in the dark
think of everyone in the dark weeping this second
of Dee the night he walked down a winter road alone
or the night he died

how the morning he died I woke up suddenly groaning
looked towards the river whispering
please dear God today help my son not have to struggle so

how his death was how my prayer was answered
how he is at last at peace – I have faith in that

how he called to me and I was there with him that
very second of his last breath

yes, I need to switch the channel
as G has taught me over and over again.

Okay – another time to a hotel room up North
a man on a phone, drunk, begging someone to come over
finally hanging up crying at first then – singing half the night

singing songs in Inuktitut
until he fell asleep
laughing

he didn't lose the music
you can't lose the music, mister

Right now mister I'm stuck praying for you
for this whole
damn sad world like I did when I was that little girl on Johnson
Avenue
beaming into the windows of the hospital.

Don't know how long Mister cries
how long I practice
tonglen giving and receiving.

Perhaps we fall asleep together.

In the morning I hear him shower, zip things, and pack, click shut,
roll his baggage across the floor, leave.

In the breakfast room, a few minutes later
there's a man alone eating
he coughs
I recognize the sound.

He looks a little like the actor whatshisname
on that television show *Breaking Bad*
respectable but a little worn around the edges
And I think *breaking sad.*

How the face we put on to function in the world
never really or rarely is the face of who we are.

Never.

How we never see ourselves as others see us, either.

How it doesn't fucking matter really
who thinks what of whom.

I catch his eye.

He looks away because he knows I know
he knew I was there when I got up to pee and flush
he would have heard me
yes it's as if we've shared
some kind of otherworldly one-night stand.

Thin walls. Thin places.

Same, maybe.

So I'll switch hotels today

where I can hear nothing.

So I will sleep and dream

try to forget

try to get this down

o all you suffering struggling souls o all you in your dark and
lonely places

o all you wiping tears away and putting on a face

you must not lose the music

you won't always be this sad

you won't always be this sad

you won't always be this sad

living in liminal worlds

you know thin places are in

parking lots waiting rooms

not just verdant fields

you are and always have been

on a threshold

spirits are everywhere

now just sit down
hush
be still
listen
long enough
to hear

The strumming of a guitar
barking of a dog
whatever is or is not
here now

now
in each breath

all I know and unknow

I knead

I read

the moss
on the side of every tree
follow the way it is growing
keep going towards

that North Star

This, another week of hibernation
of deep-sea diving into solitude and the stillness of snow
of sliding over ice fields
gathering frozen brush
until I find a bouquet for the table as beautiful as blossoms
in spring.

Raw cold snaps and fire crackles as morning's sun lights up snow
kisses trees
later we drive past woods sifted with icing sugar
round bales of hay giant white marshmallows filling the fields
promise summer.

Yes, we can, can we
imagine how a new season of imagining might begin.

I want to know
how it is
you go on living
when you've lost your child

I want to know
how it is
you can find courage enough
to face losing your husband,
the love of your life, your rock
your *anam cara*,
slowly
as he forgets more
more often

I want to know
how it is
despite your sadness and your fear
you discover
that beauty and kindness
can both kill and save you
that love and joy
can both surround and surprise you
that you can laugh

I want to know
how it is
you learn to live fully
with the wounds
with the not-knowing
and still remain ever grateful

I want to know
how it is
your screams at death
can be louder
than your screams
in giving birth

I want to know
how it is
you keep wanting to know

I want to know
how it is
you keep finding the music

I want to know
how it is
you still know
you are blessed
held
kissed by angels
while you sleep

I want to know
how it is
you begin
to inhabit
this new world
this shimmering
thin place
in peace

Do what you need to do
when you need to do it

see what you need to see
when you need to see it

say what you need to say
when you need to say it

              eat breakfast for supper

spend hours in the tub

              go to those places

that abandoned dirt road

              where you met once by chance

or was it?

that place on that road

where you got out of your car

asked him to open his door

so you could hug him

all you could do was say

              I love you I love you

over and over

– how are you?
– how do you think I am? my son is dead.

It's not how are you
more like
who are you

who are you **now**?
my **NOW** is a no and an ow
N-O

OW.

Full of pain this now
full of no it cannot be like this

So empty out: find the luminous emptiness to fill the canyon carved
in the place where a womb once was

Someone asked me the other day if I was still sad and I told her to fuck off. Yes, I did. I have a kind of Tourette syndrome brought on by death. She didn't mean to hurt me. I just think she did not want me to be sad. I don't like myself right now. I don't trust myself right now.

E tells me this state of mind one could call

instead of unstable

a kind of emotional incontinence

yes, yes, perfect because

expletives erupt
quite often
from even the sweetest lips
in grief
gush into
conversation
and oh the firecracker **FUCK**s that pop up
out of anywhere

if I were on TV
I'd be bleeped

perhaps I've become that guest
never invited back to the party

Should I say I'm sorry
I am a bit testy these days –
cranky? It's so not you, it's me.

No mystic: a misfit.

Should I confess
I am not my best self
I am my beast self
that sorrow has unleashed
a snarling sabre-toothed tigress
that I resent the
well-meaning advice
most grief books offer
by those who've suffered loss
and learned the passage of time will help ease the pain I'm in
now.

Because **now** is **now.**

my **NOW** is a no and an ow

– oh, am I repeating myself?

dead dead dead
get it through my head head head
flick a fucking switch instead
find another book you haven't read
go back to bed bed bed

– perhaps talking to a grief counsellor would help
– seriously?

I'll offer this counsel for anyone in the now of sorrow
before you book that talking session?

go to the shower
a soundproof room
your car

come with me let's go down by the ocean
scream every profanity
you ever knew and be original
make some up

blow away the wind with your swearing song
blare it out with hurricane force
that will whip the waves into whirlpools
that will whirl away venom
you never knew you had
that you pray will never come
to poison you again

up until right now you now understand
you never really knew what anger meant

yes we the undone
let's go down by the ocean and scream THIS:

I am a heart storm
I am the tornado and the hurricane
I am the blizzard and the cyclone
I am the fiery breath of the Mama Dragon
I am the fierce growl of Grandmother Bear
I will roar and keen
I will dwell in the in between
Until I can whisper

I am the soft breeze breath of Love

As my life unfolds filled with all its

Curious, mysterious, wondrous

Challenging, heart-ripping, tear-dripping moments

Ever unpredictable, messy mixedness, how can

Peace drop slow, settle in my soul as old poets and prophets
    promised and so wisely foretold?

To everything there is a season, yes, yes

A great turn of phrase, a song, a thought, but what of my cracked-
    open heart, Oh God?

No answer, really, so I dwell and live in unknowingness, in Divine
    Calendar time

Creating, waiting, loving enough to keep waiting, listening, creating
    until – yes!

Everything comes to one in an Alleluia second and peace, a
    hummingbird for now, appears!

Walking in the woods today
I stubbed my toe
looked down

there
between the shadows of poplar trees
surrounded by shrivelled leaves

was a stump

an almost perfect
heart-shaped face
smiled up at me
saying look look!
how love is all around
how it is love will find you
trip you if it has to
wake you up
remind you of beauty
over and over and over
and over. Again.

Pine needles
fine small perfect brooms
sweep through
heart darkness
whisk in light
make room for wonder

ever, wonder.

Outside, a navy blue velvet sky.
I've just put on the kettle for tea.
lit the candles in the angel candle holders
he gave me when he was eight.

Wicks catch fire, flames leap.

Hello, my son. Hello.

"Before you know what kindness really is, you must lose things."
— NAOMI SHIHAB NYE

Dear Naomi,

Sometimes, contained within one verse
is enough truth to change a universe
enough courage to win wars
words that murder us awake

yes to know kindness as the deepest thing inside you must know
sorrow as the other deepest thing

but over and over and over again the sorrows come
we lose everything and are dead by the side of the road
embrace our white ponchos

inevitable, necessary, beautiful

even kindness kills all you thought you knew for sure
one day you get it and begin again

like the first page of a new book

like a holy fool in April

A mother who didn't see the sun for a month

now plants son flowers

makes a fort between the rows

makes a bed

remembers the time

when time stopped

the planet in its spinning slide sideways

and everyone slid off the edge and there she was

all alone

the last survivor and heard a voice

Lay your burden down my child

Green is the smell of beginnings again

Lay your burden down.

This apple tree in the dreamery

is ancient twisted bent

split three ways

broken wide open

still it blooms every spring

bears fruit in the fall

our tree of life

Poetry in every rattle ramp; creak

shake of rafters, scrape of branches, groan of trees

wind roars and howls its dark dramatic symphony

blessed are the trees outside the window who breathe for me

blessed is the river which still holds the echo of my screams

reflection of my shattered dreams

blessed mother who lost her son

Mother Mary speak to me

your words of wisdom.

Early morning
glitter-sparkle
over a frosted landscape
all silver-shimmer
every step
you tread on
such sacred ground
land that needs your tending
a little while longer, yes?
love's labour
evident in pastures, fields, and trees
solid in the rocks, both whole and broken open
but there – after you have walked
Dee's labyrinth
returning to your heavy day ahead –
see the way light beams
catches
in your throat
a beckoning
you see everywhere among
those sharp and still bare
branches
reminders of some
resurrection song.

(I AM) The lone shrivelled apple
left on this tree
I still offer beauty
look at my wrinkles
softness
keep a laser gaze
upon
my fragility
because
here I still am
having held fast during
hurricane winds, rainstorms, blizzards
here I still am
until plucked
never forget
how strong
heart softness can be
how a solitary life
is
still-life
messy
juicy, even.

St. Francis,
neck-deep in snow
an ancient
golden apple
an orb
above me
together, we whisper
make us an instrument of thy peace.

A snow angel
with the wingspan
of generations
wings fanned
by my grandchild
connecting
heaven to earth

A dazzling
jazzy bling
winter singing
a happy song
under sun's warmth
a glittery snow blanket
studded with millions
of crystals
blinding anyone
everyone
who
looks upon me
but look
yes
guess

(I AM) Love

I AM.

The land, yes it's the land
that holds our stories holds us all
each delightful shriek each moan of lonliness and agony
each ecstatic moment
alleluias murmurings ululations

The land absorbs our tears until so waterlogged
worker angels must descend
to wring out mountains meadows
tundras deserts forests all the prickly cacti
until new waterfalls rivers brooks streams lakes seas
appear a mix of angel blood and human tears
                    do not despair

this earth cradles each of us like a hammock
if we rest a while in the hug and hum
each moment offers

when I lay down in green pastures
between two apple trees
where oyster shells chime a symphony
yes over and over all I hear
Handel's Lascia ch'io pianga
the soundtrack to truths I'm living now
but still
it's as if new galaxies burst forth beneath me
distant worlds where fairies sprites and pixies plot
light campfires which birth stars
which bloom into sad and tender hearts
warrior hearts that will save the planet
if we do not surrender
that will save your life *if*

you do not go under
sink in the quicksand of sorrow

        – remember, mama, you can't lose the music

I know now always knew this means the all of it
that to keep going, even in the dark
means be still hear the heart beat song of land the roar of sea
keep open open open open
hear THE MUSIC

for the music IS everywhere
music IS the blinding light, the shadows, seasons, the land
the wind oh the winds
Spirit IS music IS
everything that shimmers.

I have faith in Mystery

The God of my understanding
is a god
who sends angels
earth angels
angels to gather your ashes
angels to scatter your ashes across the seas
angels to kiss your fevered brow
with their feathery breath
maple-sugar sweet
angels who come in the night
to save your lives
trust me, there are...

because if you are here, reading this
there are angels I tell you
legions of angels
earth angels everywhere

and you and I
are born again
right now
this instant

every word between us
a star a spark

See! Listen!
You can hear the drumming
all the shining heartbeats
in black night's darkness
burning...

all the angels hovering, humming –

what more proof do we ever need?

turbulence-tossed

almost drowning in loss

until surfacing screeching

heart-bursting breaching

on the back of a whale

I sail onwards

Mary comes again comes in her blue robe a star over her heart, and she says clearly, you see, and you know what you see, so now is the season of wheelbarrow and shovel. Go through the mucky stuff, unload, get rid of the extra.

Purge!

She gives me a rose which turns into a labyrinth.
I embrace the labyrinth within.

Can I lift up my eyes
to an endless sky
raise my arms in praise
and thanksgiving
Upwards, onwards
inwards, outwards
Can I remain steady
as oak branches
despite winter's
violent winds
Can I taste the blue
swallow sun's love-light
stay
ready to eager to
receive
hear
THE MUSIC
and
whatever's next?
Yes, Yes, Yes.

I have faith!

I can shout

Rejoice

A few weeks after
– Oma, mud makes me happy.
– Mud makes me happy too. Why does it make you happy?
– Daddy work in the mud. Daddy work in the garden.
We puddle-splash the rest of the way home.

A few weeks ago
– I want to go to Daddy's labyrinth.
Even though we've just had a storm
the path's covered
and I'm afraid
of icy patches
I let her go in by herself
stand apart as she
trudges trudges trudges
reaches the centre
hugs the stone
lies down
puts her feet up on the rockface
all of this in silence.
When I join her,
her eyes are closed
she is smiling
as if she knows a secret

Afterwards, we make angels.
So simple, really.

Also, we watch *Mary Poppins*
yet another Mary who saves us.

Chim-chimney.

Super-cali-FRAGILE-is-tic.

We love to laugh. HAHAHAHA.

I have faith in children. Always.

And MERRYMERRYMERRYMARY Poppins.

Whimsy's ears perk up and her head cocks sideways

Stares up with such unconditional love

Yes, Dee looks at me through

eyes of G.O.D. (good old dog)

my pup my new big slobberingclumsygoofy pup.

One month before the anniversary, Dog saves me.

Did I ever tell you gods are dogs are gods?

Walking around the weeping willow
we planted for Dee last spring
over beside the labyrinth
I see a set of footprints
that are not mine
but there they are
frozen in the snow
leading to the woods.

Yes, I wonder
who's passed by
so glad there were others
or even AN other.

Then I turn back
to my turning
there, in the web
of winter branches
a cross of twigs
nestled in a silhouette.

Christ before me
snow drifts make it appear
perhaps, even,
an angel
watching…

call it magical thinking

bring it on

Blake said imagination is divine.

Divine Creator:

Surround this spinning planet
Surround each precious soul
Surround me as I surrender
Surround, abide, enfold.

Trust

a

word

a starburst

in

my

heart.

Standing wherever I am

with arms outstretched

in complete surrender

to what was

what is

what might come

takes as much courage

as it does faith

I am not a fearless warrior woman charging forth,

no, but slow is good. Learning to stand first is good.

– how many children do you have?

– two.

I am still the mother of two sons.

– where do they live?

One lives in Halifax

The other one

died

                        but he still is

                he is Star stuff dustinthewind

he sparkles he lives

I am broken bits of clay
last year's shards of garden pots
stacked up against
the crumbling shingled shed
beside abandoned fishing nets
the compost bin

I am sorrow softening
fertilizer for the
futile soul
when restless
that rich fresh soil
beneath the snow
knuckles of green
pushing towards the light
if you crouch down
look close enough
dare to trust enough

I am this morning's sun
above the snow fields
slowly spraying buttery light
across the blueing sky

I am that crow, its caw
that cock-a-doodle-do
that solitary pine
searching for my lost pine cone
that weeping willow smiling
at the rock
in the centre of the labyrinth
or is that a sundial marking days

I am a whirligig
of bronze-cast butterflies
that bright red
wagon
still half submerged
in snow on the front lawn
(is that perhaps
vermillion that gash-gold vermillion!)

I am those four trees
he planted
not so long ago
rooted deeper now

I am these empty garden beds
still blanketed with snow
waiting for the thaw

This woman is new earth
in God's wheelbarrow

I don't know how to
be sure of anything
really,
not my own voice
or even what I might
encounter in the next moment
let alone tomorrow
how to find certainty enough
to live with the uncertainty
that certainly lies ahead

I'm not trying to be clever
or coy
or play with words
no – not really
just saying
I no longer know how to
pretend I know
anything

all I can do
is love this man
I love
in his forgetting

learn how to say
that I'm afraid
to even admit
how afraid I am

Embrace the labyrinth within
for you see and you know what you see
remember all those yellow butterflies
you are earth in God's wheelbarrow

For you see and you know what you see
in your cone of pining
you are earth in God's wheelbarrow
still blanketed with snow

In your cone of pining
remember all those yellow butterflies!
still blanketed with snow?
embrace the labyrinth within.

Even when the sun is hidden

    snow melts to ice then water

        now these fields become my rivers

            these boots become my boat

                these outstretched arms my oars

                    this soul a deep-sea diver

each surfacing,
        each breath,
                a resurrection.

Those four trees
Dee planted
not so long ago
are rooted deeper now

These empty garden beds
still blanketed with snow
just waiting for the thaw

Perhaps Dee's new earth
in God's wheelbarrow.

I spot another trail
off the trail I am already on
one I think might be
a shortcut to the shoreline
I hope to reach

I can hear the ocean's roar

Eagerly I jump a ditch
plunge through stunted
brittle winter brush
as the wind howls
its beckoning

A few minutes later
entangled
in a thicket of brambles
I scan the bushes
dismayed to discover
the way is blocked

Then I look down

There it is:

achingly exquisite
a tiny empty nest
woven in amongst
blood red thorns
perfectly
camouflaged
bits of things
empty seed pods

string
feathers
telltale
signs of life
once lived there
most certainly
a mother with her babes

I turn back

towards the retreat house
convinced
I hear her voice
whispering:

There is no shortcut
to the shoreline of acceptance
you yearn for, anxious child,
that place of no more pain
you know (full well) does not exist
so rest just rest
I am your shoreline
I am your nest

I remember how I always loved the word nidify
To make a nest

God as nest

Then I am
alone
again

So my loves
there is howl of wind
roar of sea
gifts of kindness
so much beauty
along the way
always right there
always within our grasp

Yes
even when
the nest is empty
even when
the only way forward
is the way back
even when
the only
reason
I need a nest now
is for gathering
bits of myself
for remembering
for growing
strong enough
to fly again

The moments
I wake to birdsong
my everyday chirp choir
symphony surround sound
chickadee crow
wild geese honks for humour
hear G beside me, stirring in his sleep
look out up beyond my window
where morning sky yawns over a river, ah, this river
spoons the shoreline
a gentle lover
has always been will ever be
the river which held my screams my tears

The moments
I follow the river's curves and loops
up to the old train bridge
light my candles on the small shrine
gaze into Dee's eyes in the photo
read the postcard found at random

Hi Mom, I'm fine, it reads
and I know he is – and free.

The moments I gather
one old small dog
one big goofy puppy
who I love but the old dog?
still, not so much
laugh out loud
as she tumbles down the stairs
to greet the day
all hiya love ya
with her slurps her waggy tail *hello!*

The moments
I inhale the coffee grinds
pour water push brew
peel the orange
cross the road
where rooster crows
where donkey brays
where horses shudder
where lambs bleat
where blackflies bite
where dew sparkles

where I walk the labyrinth

that moment in that centre
when I can say
thank you thank you for the all
ALL of it

Let me tell you now it's October and we've just returned from Cape Breton after being with friends who've held us for days, with meals and boat rides and walks and talks and love. And some magic, too. Let me tell you now it's October when they finally call from the coroner's office eight months of waiting every night every day, wondering how how how how

she apologizes for the delay but called instead of making us wait longer for the letter

again a voice a cushion of kindness.

Cause of death: pneumonia *not suicide no overdose* he went to sleep and never woke up his body gave out

now I hear him saying again what he said in January

you know Mum I've done a lot of damage to my body

Did he know did he know

I run to the labyrinth then my legs give out so I crawl on my belly around each twist and turn crawl to the centre where the earth holds me as the earth ever will where my tears soak the grass where the birds are still singing

chick a dee dee dee

you know mama you can't lose the music

Death is not death it matters how a person dies it matters how a soul lived and died what images those left behind have to hold or erase about the final moments pain is pain is pain is pain is pain as relieved as I am that we can tell his children he didn't die by his own hand he died trying travelling towards the light even as I gulp for air let out all that I have swallowed in and down for seven months weep realizing how many others will not get relief weep because of the agony of others. Sorrow could kill a person if this is what some omnipotent god sees and feels God must be taking some serious antidepressants to stay alive so yes I weep guilty tears of gratitude for my gift of a different ending weep because there is no going back now to any kind of world I knew before what did I think knowing would do? When the letter comes I touch it like it's poison stare at it

– you don't have to open it, he says in whisper

I do, though.

My heart bursts into flames

there it is in black and white

                        my son my son my son is dead

             I take

          my last breath

die to the me

    I

once

was

remember the time

all night long

you'd feared his death

you'd called the police

– he's been so depressed

– he's missing again

– it's his...birthday

But then he texted

I'm sorry don't worry

so you prayed make it so

then there he was on that road

he came back

and he said Mum, Mum it's okay I'm okay

I love you too

Now remember how many times

you responded

with love not anger

even when others called you weak

you knew how strong it was

to love no matter what

think of all the wisdom

you learned from another Mary

named Libby who taught you

to storm the heavens

send legions of angels

"stay close but out of the chaos"

that man in the parking lot

who said just love him in all his

fuckedupedness

Pema who taught you the difference

between compassion

and what

Chögyam Trungpa Rinpoche

termed idiot compassion

how both your sons

taught you how to love

no matter what

think of the moment his laughter

flooded the house

when you were reading

the Tibetan Book of the Living and Dying and the Bible

trying to find rituals to send him on his way

and he said Mama

I'm dead and you're

still trying to help me

give it up, already

my mama

how you know what you heard

now go stand

in that place, on those tiles

in the kitchen

where he said

Mama all you need is a good hug

for yes, he will hug you there

always

do not listen
to the voices
that tell you
not to listen to
these kind of voices

no matter what

this is a sanity beyond all sanity

granted only to the truly undone

au·bade /ōˈbäd/ *noun*: a poem or piece of music appropriate to
the dawn or early morning

Well, we try
try to welcome every pilgrim here
even those we'd rather not
those arriving
in the shock of grief
the aftermath of sorrow
knocking at our hearts
armed with bags of dirty laundry
blisters on their feet
that need tending

sure, we have a choice
we could duck down
hide behind the curtains
pretend we're not at home
but ah – their loud insistent voices
their crude, rude manners!
they barge in hungry
say, what's for dinner?
didn't you know we'd
reach you one day?
play us some music!
they're a rowdy bawdy
unpredictable
bunch of pirate pilgrims
not unlike
Chaucer's motley crew

so yes, we try to welcome them
though they rattle our bones,
shake loose our teeth,
we are never the same
when they leave
we might even grieve them
(a little)
because what comes next – well,
the invisible pilgrims arrive
ones we cannot name or see
but know they are there
real as the clouds the mist
the whispers of angels
reminding us
we are the pilgrims
knocking on Spirit's door
let us in!
o yes, we are the hungry
this threshold is home

My mother was right
she isn't, always
only as mothers are – almost always
but she was right
when she told me
you won't always be this sad
for now, this is what I know
I am sad
and I will be sad
but it will be a different kind of sad
softer as she said
        There will be days I will be
ambushed by sorrow that brings me to my knees again
     I will rush to the labyrinth
     I hope never crawl it again
the miracle is
        I can be Alleluia joyful too
I know how joy floods into empty space
     joy as a shock of fireworks
exploding in my belly
     gratitude as the deepest thing

release receive return rejoice
       yes my friend I cannot forget to say
we the undone
       can still rejoice

Once I trekked
up a mountain
to a temple
built on the site
where a guru
had landed
having flown there
on the back of a tiger.

When they told me that
I wanted to laugh
until I thought
of the Red Sea parting
of bushes burning
of miracles of
some long-ago writer's
wild imaginings.

I understood then
I understood.

After lighting butter lamps
for everyone I loved
the world
myself
I looked down
on the valley
so far below
realized the trek back
was as dangerous
as the journey up
how it would be necessary
to pass that place

where I
had to hug the rockface
once again

I saw
if I slipped
how far the fall to my death might be.

The way up the way in the way down or out
the path is the same...
my guide
whose name was Karma
how could I make that up
said, yes, he really did,
– one step at a time, Madame.

One step at a time
into the labyrinth and back out again

any day now
I will sprout wings
and like that tiger
fly

So much
I will never be able tell another living soul
       I cannot make
the miracles
of seeing hearing smelling tasting touching

of KNOWINGness
being born inside me
every moment
       known in words ever...
that is why we call it MYSTERY
       as close as I will ever come to telling such secrets
       is pointing to a newborn baby
smell and touch that flesh
       inhale

say look, look –
       how here
in the shrivelled face of new life
       ALL is revealed.

HUGE

The Love.

Somewhere
in the midst of this mess
must be a poem someday
After all, some famous writer
(whose name you've long forgotten)
Advised: "everything's material."
Well, perhaps that's so
if you're a vulture
feeding off the dead
picking meat
off your own bones

some things are sacred
you cannot make a poem now
because everything,
as you have come to understand
is actually *im*material

because
somewhere
in the midst of the mess of this
is only you
you meeting your own humanity
you meeting your own divinity
in a collection of moments
so dark and blinding
so joyful and absurd
that you know to survive
you must transform
each as best you can
reframe re-form
into small crystal stones
clear, blue, turquoise, green

when held up to the light
a mystery of alchemy!
Then, perhaps
you string them together
fashion your own prayer beads

perhaps others will dare
to reach out
to touch
each rounded moment
feel the pulse of
eternity's energy
truth's scorching fire
in every bead
in every blessed beam of LOVE.

One learns over time
how to love the vastness
of the firmament
the mystery
of the constellations

Now, in my sixth decade
I open my mouth
as stars rain from the sky

swallow fire
the taste is oranges
stretch out my arms
I am a tree
burst into flames

Laughing.

Shhh!
Up here...way up.
Don't you see me waving?
I live on the moon now –
so far away from yesterday
yet my friends on the moon
are many.

There are wild, exotic birds here
colours you have never seen
music you cannot imagine.

Also, William Blake
the old dead poet
who went into his garden
naked and saw angels,
yep, he's my neighbour
I met him once before
years ago
on my first visit.

We read to each other.
Yesterday, Mary Oliver arrived.

She's cranky because
there are no dogs here
or trees,
the moon's
Sea of Tranquility
is not very calm.

Still,
here on the moon
eternity's music makers
create such cacophony
a reggae band a jazzy crew
a hip hop group opera stars
folk singers
oh, and Ella Fitzgerald
Until…hush harmony
in a never-ending symphony
so many versions of a moonlight sonata

I promise you
this beamer
this dreamer will
never forget
nor ever lose the music

Shh. Shh.
Listen, it's kind of a scary tale
but I will tell you a story
the way I must now
sing my soul songs
so I might stay awake
in the darkness
of mourning
until morning arrives.

Dee is everywhere

Look my love,

There he is!

Son

dances

on the tidal river

light

bounces

Spirit's silver-shimmer

God's glory-glitter

Everywhere

ACKNOWLEDGEMENTS

I thank all who have travelled with me in person or in the world of words in our first year and beyond.

My constants, most especially, Deanne Fitzpatrick, Dawna Ring, Rita Wilson, Marie Thompson, Paula Danckert, and Whitney Moran.

To all who have sent condolences and prayers from many faith traditions, most especially Lisa Doucet, Carol Campbell-Smith, Jan Watson, Laura King and family, Catherine Martin, the Sisters of Saint Martha in Antigonish, The Sisters of Charity at Seton Spirituality Centre. All I cannot name. Prayers received.

Jean Baird, Dawn Leslie, Catherine Martin, Sheree Gilchrist, Ann Slade, Gayle Harvey, Theresa Babb, and Paula Harmon are amongst many bereaved mothers who reached out to me. My heart was and is held in their embrace. And yes, Jean, we cannnot forget the fourth R: rejoice.

I thank all who sent gifts of books, words, food, comfort, dream catchers, rocks, scarves, *laughter,* and so so much more. There are too many to list here but I need to name. Lana McEachern, Ann Slade, Deb Plestid, David Baxter, Joan Baxter, Karlheinz Eyrich, Hannah Hunnziker, Anne Simpson, Kate Inglis, Dawn Leslie, Gillian and John Crawford, Cathe MacLean, Josh Mulholland, Hilary Drummond, Mary Jo Anderson, Shelley Ambrose, Kathleen Broyles and James Pagel, Lee Muir Buckley and Sadie and Piper, Cassie MacGregor.

I'm blessed with a wonderful community of writers. Thanks Peggy Atwood for your gift of poetry. Chris Benjamin and Catherine Martin for letting me use their words to me. I thank Isabelle Allende and Jean Shinoda Bolen for gracious correspondence. Beth Powning for her knowing. Meg Wolitzer for her texts and phone calls. For inviting me into their writing circle, Anne Simpson, Rita Wilson, Rosario Campbell. Harry Thurston, for listening as only you can, during our stay at Sherbrooke Village.

As weirdly wired as this world is, to my friends in the land of social media, you sustained me often. Made me braver to share and complete this work.

To all who "Saw" my son and treated him with compassion. Pharmacists, nurses, social workers, doctors. Earth angels. I give thanks for you every day.

To those in my village who gave Dee respect and work when needed. Dianne Shink, Terry Reid, the late Roger McClellan. Dear Roger, I hope you and Dee are shooting the breeze and saving fox babies. Valri Suidgeest and family for dropping by. Nancy Langille for knowing she had to come. And James Charuk, for your timely re-entry in my life and generosity.

I am so grateful to Norma Bailie for bravely showing up when she did and her magical Peppermint Patties. For her hugs and heart. Carol Blundon for her endless support and friendship but especially appearing with hamburger soup at a crucial moment. Who knew hamburger soup could be lifesaving? Kathleen Power for keeping me strong in so many ways and always understanding.

To Paulette and Bob Fowler, Joan MacKeigan, David Boes, and especially Linda Little for all you did and do to help us keep Mabel Murple's Book Shoppe and Dreamery keeping on. To all our vistors, you were medicine. Thank you for letting me hug your babies. Some day, a happy book called *The Dreamery*!

To my friends at Atlantic Independent Booksellers Association for your kindness beyond the beyond, to Starr Cunningham and Nova Scotia Mental Health Foundation, Nimbus team, most especially Karen McMullin, Tika Jakobsen, and Emma FitzGerald, who, along with Dawna Ring, got me through New York. Dawna, you are My Dawn – Madonna. Let's keep dancing.

My immediate family: sister Leanne, my mother, Doe Fitch, my husband, Gilles Plante, and my son Jordan McCormack. My grandchildren, all our Quebec family and friends. Regis Labeaume and Daniel Lavoie. To Chosen family, Sara McElman, Alana Desorcy, Hollie Millington, Britanny Leblanc.

To Carol MacDougall, Jennifer Henderson and Costas Halavrazos, Blair Maher, for friendship always but who, along with Lillian and Julia Weir, Stefanie McCormack, and David Myles, offered so much in a time of shock.

To Kristine MaCutcheon and community at Dorje Dema Ling and my Dancing Tara Friends. O the gift of that weekend. To Josette Coulter and Kirsten Elizabeth Langille and groovy goddesses for all the magic.

To The Abbey of the Arts community, the online retreats and study I was somehow led toward. Christine Valters Paintner and John Valters Paintner, the work you do is THE WORK. To Libby Cataldi and the Stay Close community for so many years of wisdom and guidance and hope. I am graced with guidance of Melissa Gayle West, her labyrinth work and wisdom. I am ever learning the wild dance of this life. You are, to me, a Mary, a She Who Knows.

To Emily Stewart, who was a godsend and helped get me to where I dared to press send to Whitney, and Cory Pacione for speedy creative input when asked. To Michele Porter for kind first eyes.

Last of all, the critters at Happy Doodle Do and Brian Clarke who helps us with those critters. And seriously, Oscar the sheepdog, Whitney and Dave's spirit animal, who led me to Fundy Sheepdogs, where Heather Olsen led me to my Whimsy. My Dog! My Dog! Leadeth me to stiller waters. Another beating heart. Such music to my ears.

SUGGESTIONS FOR FURTHER READING

Music worked best for me, but here are a few titles from a year of reading or re-reading sadly, madly, gladly, sporadically.

A Grief Observed by C. S Lewis, Faber and Faber, 2012.

Anam Cara: A Book of Celtic Wisdom by John O'Donohue, HarperCollins, 1997.

A Year With Rilke translated and edited by Joanna Macy and Anita Barrows, HarperColins, 1996.

Beauty: The Invisible Embrace: Rediscovering the True Sources of Compassion, Serenity, and Hope by John O'Donohue, HarperCollins, 2004.

Connemara Blues by John O'Donogue, HarperCollins, 2001.

Devotions: The Selected Poems of Mary Oliver, Penguin, 2017.

Exploring the Labyrinth: A Guide for Healing and Spiritual Growth by Melissa Gayle West, Random House, 2000.

God in all Worlds: An Anthology of Contemporary Spiritual Writing, Random House, 1995.

God's Fool: The Life and Times of Francis of Assisi by Julian Green Carver, Harper and Row, 1987.

Holy Bible

How the Gods Pour Tea by Lynn Davies, Goose Lane Editions, 2013.

Lament for a Son by Nicholas Wolsterstoff, Eerdmans, 1987.

Living Buddha, Living Christ by Thich Nhat Hanh, Riverhead Books, 1995.

Michael Rosen's Sad Book, Walker Books, 2010.

Miracles by C. S. Lewis, HarperCollins, 2001.

Mirror of the Simple Soul by Marguerite Porete, Soul Care Publishing, 2012.

Once More We Saw Stars by Jayson Greene, Alfred A. Knopf, 2019.

Polly MacAuley's Finest, Divinest, Wooliest Gift of All by Sheree Fitch (*read out loud*), Running the Goat Books & Broadsides, 2018.

Rilke's Book of Hours translated by Anita Barrows and Joanna Macy, Riverhead books, 2005.

That Crisp Day Closing on my Hand: The Poetry of M. Travis Lane by M. Travis Lane, Wilfrid Laurier Press, 2007.

The Cloud of Unknowing edited by William Johnston, Doubleday, 1973.

The Gift: Poems by Hafiz, the Great Sufi Master translated by Daniel Ladinsky, Penguin, 1999.

The Heart Does Break: Canadian Writers on Grief and Mourning edited by George Bowering and Jean Baird, Random House Canada, 2009.

The Holy Book of Women's Mysteries by Zsuzsanna Ermese Budapest, Susan B Anthony Books, 1980.

The Instruction Manual for Receiving God by Jason Schulman, Sounds True, 2006.

The Soul in Balance: The Gardens of Washington National Cathedral by Alexandra Scott Heidi Read Isabel Scott, Epm Pubns Inc, 1998.

The Soul's Slow Ripening: 12 Celtic Practices for Seeking the Sacred by Christine Valters Paintner, Sorin Books, 2018.

The Tent by Margaret Atwood, Doubleday. 2006.

The Tibetan Book of Living and Dying by Sogyal Rinpoche, Random House, 1992

Upstream by Mary Oliver, Penguin, 2016.

Welcoming the Unwelcome: Wholehearted Living in a Brokenhearted World by Pema Chodron, Penguin, 2019.

Zen Keys: A Guide to Zen Practice by Thich Nhat Hanh, Doubleday, 1995.